PHOTOGRAPHY
MANUAL

Valentina Leu

FROM BEGINE
TO IMPACT
PHOTOS

Do you get when use your camera?
In few steps I can teach you to use it to the fullest.

Manual for analogic and digital photography

Index:

THE ORIGINS OF PHOTOGRAPHY

Now the picture has more than a century but never in its history had undergone a transformation so deep as happened with the advent of digital photography.

At the beginning, a photography was an event that whole families could not afford; how many photos we have of our great-grandparents?

How many of our family photos from the period before the Second World War? Maybe a handful of photos taken in very special occasions.

Even with the advent of 35mm format, typical of common photographic films, photography has in fact become a way of expression for everyone.

However, until recent times, the photography has remained linked to the traditional process of chemical development.

The 35mm camera

With the exception of a few large photo enthusiasts who bought films meters and derived their in home bathroom a homemade darkroom for development in their own photos, it was necessary to take pictures of an entire roll of film and then go to a photo lab that provided to develop and print the photos (or the development and framework of slides for those who preferred this type of support).

Any decision concerning the shoot could follow two paths.

It could take a photo in full manual mode, in which case, relying on its experience, the photographer had to set the speed, aperture, and other shooting options (such as zoom and focus) hoping, based on the conditions of light, to get the result he has in mind.

Much more often he wore the eventual selector shooting mode to an automatic position and then left that the camera was preoccupied with everything else.

The reality is that all those who have had some experience of using a traditional camera, film, certainly took memorable photographs, but in some cases have even got terrible results:

-Photos completely "burned" (white or clear) or too dark, due to an incorrect timing; other times just after the release that we discovered a photograph that must certainly beautiful was really moved.

The film

A key factor in the case of traditional photography is the film.

The camera roll, for prints or slides, is constituted by a support of transparent plastic material, on which is deposited a jelly of chemical substances sensitive to light, which allow to fix for always the result of a shot, exposure to light .

There were, and still are, high and low quality films.

Once again, the only way to really make sure of the results was to go to a photo lab, leave the film for develop and print and wait patiently.

The presence of the film introduces enormous costs. For those who were accustomed to using only two or three rolls of film a year, the cost could be acceptable, but those who want to retain a memory of more or less important events of his life or a trip, he would face a considerable expense, between the cost of the rollers and the next stage of development and printing.

The peculiarities of digital photography

Digital photography has revolutionized the way of taking pictures. Now we can finally take a photo and view the result immediately, down to the smallest details, so we can decide whether or not to keep shooting. Having eliminated the costs of purchase of the roller and development costs, every single shot does not cost. With analogic photography, only on special occasions we could hear the phrase "Take another shoot, you never know." Today, thanks to digital photography, because they take a single picture, when we taking new two, three or even ten? Indeed, given that not always observing the small display normally present on the back of photo camera it is possible to take full advantage of the strengths and weaknesses of a photo, it is always good practice to run multiple shots, to increase the probability to capture a significant expression or fun.

Basically we can use a digital camera wherever we want and whenever we want, without spending constraint. The only real cost to deal with for taking digital photographs is the purchase of the camera and a memory card. Not always, however the memory card is supplied with the machine, when then is supplied, it will invariably minimum capacity and generally offer the possibility to realize only a handful of shots. Because, presumably, the digital camera will be with us for a long period of time, it is best to learn how to choose the device with caution.

THE TECHNIQUE

The term "photography", from photo (light) and graphy (writing), reveals the basic element on which is based every photographic technique: light.

So to understand the photography we have to start right from the light.

The light enters from 'camera lens and crosses its lens system, which focuses the image on a plane placed at the back of the photo camera and called focal plane (Figure 2.1)

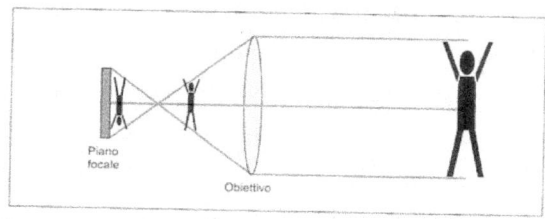

Figura 2.1 La luce entra dalla lente frontale dell'obiettivo. L'obiettivo mette a fuoco l'immagine, capovolta, sul piano focale della fotocamera, esattamente nel punto in cui si trova la pellicola o il sensore CCD o CMOS.

The analogic photography

In analogic camera, the image flowing on the focal plane.

After pressing the button, the camera opens the shutter; at this point the light reaches the surface of the photographic film.

In a photographic film, the frame is constituted by a transparent support made of plastic material, covered by a layer of gelatin, inside of which are found in suspension of silver salts crystals.

The black and white

Know the Operational of films in black and white is useful to understand the color photography.

The exposure to photons of light, due to the shutter, produces in 'photographic emulsion a reaction. On the film is formed in this way a latent image, that during the development process can be revealed and made visible through the application of appropriate chemicals.

Color photography

In a color film it is used three layers of sensitive material, quite similar to those used for photography in black and white.

Each of them is sensitive to different colors, or to different wavelengths of light.

The layer closer to the light source is sensitive only to shorter wavelengths, corresponding to blue light.

Below it is a sensitive layer only to the medium wavelengths, corresponding to the green light.

Finally there is one sensitive layer only at longer wavelengths, corresponding to red light.

Therefore, on the surface of a photographic film are formed three monochrome images (ie black and white) superimposed, as if it were three black and white films placed one above the other.

The technique of digital photography

Digital photography has many similarities and many differences compared to traditional photography.

In a digital camera instead of a film there is an electronic sensor. The most commonly used types of sensors are CCD and CMOS.

The importance of light

Regardless of the technology used to acquire the image (analogically on film or digitally through an electronic sensor) it is evident that the very essence of photography consists of the acquisition of the reflected light from the classified elements.

It is therefore essential that the light strikes the sensitive element is neither too much nor too little (Figure 2.14).

Overexposed

Suppose you have set your camera in manual mode and choosing an over-shooting time. On a digital camera, the sensor will be hit by the light coming from the scene framed for an excessive time, collect an excessive number of photons and sometimes reach or exceed its maximum capacity acquisition. In this way each photo sites announce that she had received almost the maximum amount of light. This situation is equivalent to "read" the white color, as the brightness will be highest along the color spectrum. Photo will be overexposed in this case, that is too light, and the limit will be completely white.

Underexposure

The opposite situation occurs when the ambient brightness is low and choose a slower shutter speed too fast. In this case, the photosites collect low quantity of photons. Therefore information about the three primary colors are all close to zero and still too low, and this will translate into color next to black. The entire picture will therefore be very dark (Figure 2.16) or even black. In this case it says that the picture is underexposed

Time and aperture

The camera can use two methods to control the amount of light entering the lens and reaches the sensitive material: can adjust the shutter time and can adjust the aperture.

The shutter

The shutter speed determines the fraction of time in which the film or the sensor are exposed to the light conveyed by the lens. The shutter speed depends on the ambient lighting conditions.

In full sun, well-lit a subject may be exposed for a very short time, while on the other hand a panorama of a city at sunset or, more so, the photograph of the night sky will require an exposure time progressively longer.

Stretching the shutter speed beyond a certain threshold you run the risk of selecting a too long time, so that the same scene may change; a subject may move, even imperceptibly, generating a moved picture.

Timing and ambition

The shutter speed "slow" selectable without running the risk of taking photographs moves it depends on the type of lens attached to the camera. In more practical is the lens focal length (a topic that will be later) shorter treaty must be the shutter time.

When we photograph a wide scene with a wide angle, the small movements of the camera will be negligible; with telephoto lenses pushed the slightest movement of the hand will become macroscopic, increasing the chances of taking photographs moves.

The Aperture

In a camera there is a second factor that governs the amount of light that reaches the sensitive surface: the aperture. It is a group of metal plates arranged in a circle, the opening of which determines the diameter of a hole that lets through only a certain amount of light. In practice, a larger aperture will be able to spend a greater amount of light will pass, and closed diaphragm a lesser amount of light.

While the measurement of exposure times is immediately understandable, as it is still of fractions of a second, the aperture adopt a less intuitive measurement system, called fstop. In practice, this value is derived from a simple calculation that evaluates the relationship between the focal length of the lens (which will be discussed later) and the diameter of the aperture, which is the opening through which can pass the light.

The reciprocity between shutter speed and aperture

There is a reciprocal relationship between the time and aperture. We can for example take a photograph by setting the shutter speed to 1/125 second, and the aperture of F4 .In the camera enters a certain amount of light, which suppose suitable for taking a specific photograph.

But the same amount of light would enter also by setting the timing of 1/60 of a second (and therefore a double compared to the previous case time) and by setting the aperture of F5.6 (which as has been said previously, lets pass a quantity of light equal to half compared to F3.5 diaphragm). A half amount of light which, however, can enter into the camera for twice the time is equivalent to the same amount of light.

Similarly we can take the same photograph also using 1/30 of a second (twice as long compared to 1/60 and four times higher than 1/125) and setting the aperture of F8 (a size equal to half the diaphragm aperture and F5.6 a quarter of the diaphragm F4). In the room photos will always enter the same amount of light.

The result is the same? No, because there is a particular effect: the depth of field.

The depth of field

The aperture determines the range of distances from the camera in which subjects will be in focus. By choosing a very open aperture we will achieve a minimum depth of field, while choosing a very small aperture will get a much larger depth of field.

Suppose you want to achieve a portrait with a subject at about three meters away, using a particularly small aperture will get the effect of focus on both the subject and everything that lies in front and behind.

Instead choosing a very open aperture will achieve the opposite effect: the face (and sometimes only the face) of the subject will be perfectly in focus, while everything that is located in front of or behind the subject will be more or less out of focus. This will have the effect of focusing attention on the subject: photography will thus become a real portrait. Furthermore, the depth of field varies depending on the subject distance and the focal length of the lens (which will be discussed later).

The film sensitivity

The film speed is measured with ISO scale, which comes directly from the old stairs ASA, retaining exactly the same values.

For remarkable brightness conditions, a time could be purchased by rollers 64 or 50 ISO, containing little sensitive films. These films were equipped with smaller crystals of silver salts of those present on a roller 100 150. Therefore, they were able to give a photographic image of extraordinary quality, where even at high magnifications was difficult to distinguish any disturbances.

When the light is low they arise instead of problems. Assuming having to take picture with an analog camera in low-light conditions, we will provide us with a film with a much higher sensitivity to ISO standard 100, or 800, ISO 1600 and beyond.

But also the sensitivity has a price: to achieve more sensitive films, manufacturers must use larger crystals which, gradually growing the sensitivity of the film, will become particularly evident forming the phenomenon of grain, a disorder that is manifested by a reduction of the overall sharpness of the photograph. The contours of the subjects will not be sharper but jagged, undulating

The sensitivity in digital cameras

In digital cameras, the CCD sensitivity is fixed and can not be varied in any way.

In fact in a digital camera, the sensitivity control amplifier acts as a multiplicative factor which is connected to the CCD sensor.

Artificially increasing the "sensitivity" of the CCD sensor via the amplifier, there is nothing that multiply by 2, 4 and over the number of photons read by photosites transformed into electrons. When the brightness is very poor and very few photons acquired by photosites, it will generate errors, because the photosites receive very few photons, in a quantity that does not enable to accurately distinguish the actual color of the subject.

The lens

Each camera, even the simplest, is to force things with a goal. The goal is that set of lenses that converges the light towards the focal plane. It is inside the lens that is located the aperture, which will command the camera to close just before opening the shutter for shooting.

Therefore, the purpose of a goal is to converge and focus the light on the focal plane of the camera, or at the exact point at which is located the film or CCD sensor.

The focal length

The main value is to feature a lens focal length. This represents the distance between lens and the focal plane of the camera.

In this case, the transition from traditional analogic cameras to digital cameras has private photographers unit of unambiguous measurement.

The focal length of a lens depends in fact on the sensitive area dimensions on which must be focused on the subject.

Standard lenses

A standard lens has a focal length of 50 mm. A goal of this type returns a field of view of about 45 degrees, providing a substantially result comparable to the kind of vision that we offer our eyes. A standard lens does not introduce deformations of the environment and presents no particular difficulty of shooting, nor in terms of time, either in terms of depth of field.

Standard lenses are suitable a little 'for all: indoor photography, family photographs, photographs of landscapes and so on. A goal for all needs, without special skills: a good "workhorse"

Wide-angle lenses

There is talk of wide angle when the focal length falls below 50 mm. The focal length values typically used for this kind of objectives there are 15 and 28 mm, respectively, which allow to embrace a 63 and 75 degree field.

With a wide-angle lens you can be resumed with greater ease a scene in confined spaces, since the goal will enable to embrace a broader slice of the surrounding environment.

But everything has a price. Wide-angle lenses introduce of: straight lines perspective deformations that were rendered correctly by a 'standard' lens are progressively more curved from a wide-angle lens, which will introduce the deformations always more accentuated in hand to hand that it shortens the focal length.

Telephoto lenses moderate

Returning for a moment to the standard focal length of 50 mm, we can push in the opposite direction with respect to the wide-angle lenses: exceeding the threshold of 50 mm enter in the field of lenses, which have specific applications and can give great satisfaction.

A telephoto lens is able to consider a field angle more progressively reduced as compared to a normal lens. Proceeding from 50 mm, you can reach the focal lengths of 85, 100 and 135 mm. It is lightweight tele objectives, particularly suited to portraits.

A telephoto not push is ideal for taking pictures of portraits, as its depth of field, but not limited too, allows us to isolate the subject from the background without all away produce unpleasant results, in which the object remains only one element focused into picture on a completely indistinguishable background.

Increasing the focal length, you can be reached from 200 or 300 mm telephoto lenses that are beginning to be used for particular applications such as photographic hunting. Objectives of this kind allow to resume an angle of respectively 12 and 8 degrees, with the result of zoom in on distant objects and sell "closest".

It, however, also highlight the typical negative characteristics of telephoto lenses: the depth of field will often be limited, even if the subject is located at an optimal distance.

At the same time it is becoming increasingly evident another negative effect: the minimum focus distance will grow more and more difficult to be able to focus on a subject at less than a few meters away.

the brightness is also a problem: a telephoto lens "captures" the few photons it receives from a small clove of field in front of him. Consequently, the time required to take the picture are getting longer, but then a powerful telephoto not easily tolerate exposure times are too long, which invariably produce photographs moves.

The brightness of a lens

If the first characteristic of a lens is the focal length, which allows to discriminate between wide-angle, standard goals and tele objectives, the second most important characteristic of a lens is the brightness.

The brightness value indicates the maximum aperture.

The maximum aperture depends on various factors, one of which is the constructive quality of the lens. Best lens, and more expensive, will be able to provide greater brightness, while less prestigious lens can provide a lower brightness.

Intuitively, this concept is pretty clear: higher brightness equivalent to a better target.

THE DIGITAL CAMERAS

Now we know:

> - on what mechanisms underlying the operation of a camera
> - what a photograph and thanks to such chemical or electronic processes is formed
> - more clearly all the factors that revolve around a snap: exposure time, aperture, shutter, sensitivity and lens

With these informations we can deal with the added security of the operation argument itself of a digital camera.

In the previous chapter we had the opportunity to observe how the basic element of a digital camera, the CCD sensor, whose job is to capture the image, which can then turn into a file, first seen on the display, then on a computer screen and then printed on paper for a more traditional use.

Yes it is usual to assess a CCD on the basis of the resolution in a place that is able to offer, measured in megapixels (MP).

It is typically of low-end cameras, from a few MP and in general the majority of the installed cameras on mobile phones. Usually when it is given a single focal length, manufacturers prefer to adopt a moderate wide angle, offering the ability to take snapshots of landscapes or generic items such as family photographs or a group of friends.

Zoom

Almost all cameras offer the possibility of using a digital zoom. The name is intriguing, but what does that really mean? There are two zoom mechanisms: an optical and a digital. In the "optical zoom", the position of the lens inside the lens varies so as to enlarge the surface of the CCD only that part of the field which we are interested.

The "digital zoom" performs this same operation, but without changing the focal length of the lens; on the contrary considers only the central part of the image that is formed on the CCD.

Cameras with lens 3X

A goal at least 3x is now present on most compact digital cameras. A goal of this type offers a focal length with an extension that goes from a moderate wide-angle (usually about 33 mm) to a moderate telephoto (33 X 3 = 103 mm). Objectives of this extension already offer greater versatility, as they allow on the one hand to take views of satisfactory amplitude and on the other to take pictures with a telephoto lens capable of ensuring the excellent performance in the pictures of portraits and able to grasp details not too distant or unnecessary. If the resolution of the CCD is sufficient, the 8 MP up, we will also delve, in moderation, in the initial areas of the digital zoom, so l be able to approach a subject a bit 'too far,

Camera with 4X lens

Lens of this type offer added versatility than 3x. Therefore the extension of the lens focal lengths is even wider. However, this extension is only rarely offered in a balanced way between the wide-angle range and telephoto range. Typically, manufacturers offer a lens which extends from moderate wide angle (35 mm) to medium telephoto (35 X 4 = 140 mm). So is privileged the extension in telephoto, or the ability to bring distant subjects otherwise. We thus have available focal lengths from moderate wide angle, all 'standard lens, the telephoto lens for portraits and beyond.

Cameras with lens from 6X to 10X

The cameras with lenses of this type, as we have seen for cameras of the previous range, only in rare cases offer a special extension on the wide-angle range (typically start at all as a focal length of 32 mm or 35 mm), but typically offer a more stringent telephoto, with which we can see distant objects of small size, for example an architectural detail or a subject rather distant.

For example, they can be excellent for taking pictures from a distance when the children plays, without being seen, standing at a distance and pretending to fiddle with the camera: children do not think that we are actually photographing them and will play more naturally. In addition, in a landscape, a telephoto lens of this level (35 X 6 = 210 mm, 35 X 10 = 350 mm) allow to seize minutes or elements that are located at a considerable distance.

It is however also targets that begin to present problems, since we will have to struggle hard to ensure the stability of the camera to these focal lengths and sometimes we have to enlist the assistance of a tripod (or any solid support).

Cameras with more than 10X lens

The cameras with wide-zoom extents are normally bridge calls, since they act as a "bridge" between compact and DSLR. Currently the level of maximum extension reached by bridge cameras is 36x. In these cases it is more likely that the manufacturer has managed to extend the focal even in the field of wide-angle, reaching focal equivalent to 28 mm. At the other end we will have a telephoto quite striking focal length. There are many limitations to what we can do with a camera equipped with a lens of this type, which will be able to find even tiny details and distant, and will allow us to play very well to photographic safari photographs. Even without counting the Digital Zoom, we can achieve extraordinary photographs,

The Exposure meter

The meter is a system which evaluates the brightness of the image and adjusts the time and the shutter aperture.

The cheaper cameras do not offer any possibility of controlling the operation of the exposure, which guarantees only a reading of maximum and limits the speed and aperture for the shot. The best compact cameras and digital SLR cameras offer instead in general various modes.

Autofocus

The cheaper cameras are generally equipped with a lens with fixed focal length and fixed iris; accordingly allow to vary the shutter speed only. In these cases, the lens has a aperture rather closed, allowing you to focus on just about everything that is in front of all 'objective.

The regular compact cameras, however, are equipped with an autofocus system, capable of identifying the subject of the picture and lock on it the focus.

The most simple cameras only offer the automatic position, in which the apparatus, on the basis of a preset program, identify the subject of the photograph in a number of areas (usually 9, in the central area of the frame), and then put him to fire.

The white balance

The human eye is able to automatically balance the brightness of the environment, since the vision is mediated by the brain that, automatically, is able to perceive the medium shade present in the environment and adapt to its variations. So, to some extent, we are able to correctly distinguish the white color in full sun, at sunset or in an indoor environment, with any type of lighting.

The CCD is practically the eye of the camera: All camera's electronic components must be able to balance the colors detected by the CCD based on the content of the scene. For example, in a photo interior, without flash, the CCD probably detect a predominance of the yellow / red hues typical of illumination produced by incandescent lamps (tungsten). The camera's logic will notice, however, of this condition and will automatically try to balance the colors, so as to make the white color correctly (or frost white or creamy white, but pure white).

The image saving format

The cameras can save pictures to the memory card using the JPEG compressed format. It is a format that introduces, by definition, a loss of information. In practice, the JPEG format analyzes those image elements that are not perceptible to the human eye and eliminates them by allowing you to save disk space.

All reflex cameras and even some high-level compact cameras can store images in RAW format, or in an uncompressed format, the specific camera.

Inevitably the pictures saved in RAW format have huge size; Also only a few software are able to handle this graphical format.

DIGITAL TYPES PHOTOCAMERAS

The traditional cameras were placed to the size of the roll) of the film and the frame: 36 X 24 mm; Today the manufacturer has the utmost freedom in developing a digital camera that can meet the needs of its wielder. then arises the need to find out what our real needs) to choose the model that best suits our needs.

The analog cameras

In analog photography, the camera size were determined by the size of the roll and the frame (36 X 24 mm). All analog cameras have, more or less, the shape of a parallelepiped, such as a small "box" which revolves around the area of the focal plane, where the film, ready for shooting flowing. There have always been very compact models in which all the spaces were optimized to favor size and practicality. However, miniaturization has never been able to go beyond specific physical limitations

Digital cameras

In digital cameras, the situation is radically different. The manufacturer has the utmost freedom in designing the camera and this allows him to create models also looks weird. In addition now also in mobile phones we can find photos from the performance rooms sometimes not indifferent.

The majority of cameras adopts sensors with a diagonal of about ten millimeters. This surface represents only a fraction of the size of the frame on a 35mm film.

The camera in the phone

Where once the chamber this photo in mobile phones was not particularly interesting accessory in photographic terms, because it could offer a resolution of only 0.3 MP, today is undergoing a tendency to be installed on most phones a digital camera more than satisfactory quality.

The new models are increasingly 5 MP and beyond and, at least at the level of definition, can rival the cameras' standard. "They have basically two types of problems: the difficulty of shooting in poor lighting conditions and the absence of an optical zoom.

Cameras "entry-level"

There are still several digital cameras on the market very attractive price, offers from unknown manufacturers or otherwise known to produce low-level electronic equipment.

Normally devices of this type have a very limited resolution, 0.3 to 2 MP. In some cases, however, it is declared a much higher resolution, typically obtained by interpolation techniques of the few pixels actually made available by the CCD sensor.

The advice is to avoid this type of appliance, which offer poor performance, often lower than those obtained with a camera phone

Ultra-compact cameras

There are on the market models of digital cameras to extremely compact dimensions, equal to those of a credit card or a little more and with a reduced thickness. At one time in this category existed only fixed-focus apparatus and equipped with a lens with a fixed focal length. Many ultra-compact devices offer now typical functions of a medium level camera. Almost always, the devices of this type use SD cards that offer outstanding capacity / size.

Compact digital cameras

This category includes most of the devices currently on the market. Here there is literally spoiled for choice in terms of price and performance. Many models in this class bear a certain extent, also a rather rough treatment. Currently the tendency is to provide apparatus with a resolution ranging between 6 and 12 MP. Many devices that fall into this category offer a rich set of automatic programs for special situations. Since they are of a size not particularly limited but they are not even particularly bulky, they can normally provide a zoom (optical) not greater than 6X, which will however be able to give great satisfaction.

Advanced compact cameras: the bridge models

Some compact cameras are characterized by some advanced features. For example, they can be equipped with a zoom particular extension (8x, 12x or even 20x). Moreover, this kind of cameras offers an extensive set of manual and creative settings. Many of the models fitted with special offer extended zoom optical or electronic image stabilization

A digital apparatus of this type typically offers objectives with an extension from 28 mm to 300 mm and more with the ability to further extend this excursion using special high-quality optical additional.

Cameras SLR affordable price

They represent the access point into the world of digital SLR photography. They have more or less the size of an analogue SLR camera, a 35mm film, and offer full or partial compatibility with the range of interchangeable lenses made by the manufacturer of the camera and from independent producers.

This has the added advantage of a device of this type: the possibility of using an SLR unit not too expensive and packed with features comparable to those of a professional device and at the same time the possibility of using all the previously purchased lenses park / accessories analog camera and access to the wide range of available lenses on the market.

Devices of this type do not typically offer a CCD / CMOS sensor in full format U "or of dimensions equal to those of the frame in the 35mm format.

Professional SLR Cameras

These are exceptional equipment from all points of view. These cameras use almost exclusively fast CCD or CMOS sensors in photo format 3: 2. Very often these devices on the sensor is full-frame, or has the same or next in size to those of the analog frame: 36 X 24 mm.

Even the camera body is sized based on the typical needs of a professional photographer, you may have to operate in extreme conditions, adverse or dangerous: under the weather or extreme cold or scorching, in the dust, in social crisis situations or war. The resolution offered by devices of this type is at the top of the current possibilities. Although the pixel resolution is often abused to define the quality of a room photo, it is also true that for a professional photographer the highest level of detail is always important. Devices of this type reached and in some cases exceed the threshold of 20 MP, with extraordinary detail.

RULES 'OF USE OF THE CAMERA

In general, a digital camera always provides a fully automated program, allowing you to take pictures without thoughts.

It also offers a series of semi-automatic programs, thanks to which we can set one of the exposure values (time or aperture) and let the camera automatically calculate the other value.

There are also various specialized programs, which the manufacturer has set the camera to facilitate as much as possible the realization of photographs in very specific situations.

Auto photography

It happens frequently needing or wanting to take pictures on the fly, meaning only capture a scene or a nice situation, especially significant or when we do not have the time or inclination to worry too much about the various settings offered by the camera.

Automatic location of a digital camera does just that: a "breakout" only when we want to take a picture without worrying about anything.

What happens when we use the fully automatic setting of a digital camera depends substantially on the internal processing logic that the manufacturer has inserted into the machine.

This will produce on average a correct picture, but can also lead to errors of judgment clear: what happens if the photo subject is lit differently than the rest of the scene? The camera will attempt to calculate a median exposure, with the result that a subject well lit against a dark background will certainly overexposed, but if on the contrary the subject is a bit 'in the shade of a very light background (or backlight), will appear very dark.

Even a non-intelligent autofocus, which evaluates a hypothetical general subject matter at the center of the photograph, can produce erroneous results.

When we perform the pre-shooting operation, or when we press halfway the shutter button, some cameras indicate what will be the subject of the photograph. If we notice that the camera has identified the wrong person, we ritentiamo shooting trying to better frame the true subject of the photograph.

When you choose the automatic setting

The fully automatic photography can be useful in situations where you need to take pictures "very fast."

It is an appropriate setting a bit 'all-purpose, just for the fact that it is not specialized for any particular use.

When do you not choose the automatic setting

If we have to shoot moving subjects time normally selected by the automatic mode may not be fast enough; if so invariably they produce picture moves.

When the subject is in a highly decentralized position in the composition of the photograph; even the best automated systems fail to locate it as the real subject of the photograph and focus on some other more central element.

When the subject is illuminated in a particular way and different from the context; for example in the case of a performance on a stage: the subject will be perfectly illuminated by stage lights on a dark background normally. Similarly, a subject photographed against the result invariably dark and underexposed, because the camera will attempt to calculate exposure properly even able to make the background.

Program shooting

It may seem strange that a camera there is an automatic "position" and another location "programmed"; that there are differences between these two approaches?

In automatic mode, the camera has the right to choose all the settings needed to handle shooting: shutter speed, aperture, autofocus, flash and sensitivity of the CCD.

In Program mode instead we have some possibilities of intervention. For example, we can change the autofocus employed. Some cameras fact offer more ways of assessing exposure and autofocus Center-weighted, evaluative, spot. We can then choose, for example, as a subject to focus and decide to turn off the camera flash when its use is inappropriate, or when we realize that, given the distance of the subject, the flash does not make any difference and would involve only one waste, sometimes considerable, of electricity.

When choosing the programmed setting

The programmed mode is in practice an automatic mode that gives us some possibility of intervention in addition, by exploiting the functionality of the camera.

For example, if we realize that, in the scene you're photographing, the flash would be completely useless or even harmful or unwanted, we can choose the programmed setting and then turn off the flash. Not relying on the flash, the camera will choose inevitably longer exposure time and therefore we have to take pictures with a very steady hand or with the help of a tripod, but we'll get the shot you want.

Autofocus

If we want to set the autofocus or the exposure metering method especially because the subject is in a difficult angle or is lit in a very different way of context, choose the programmed mode and use the camera's settings to enable it to identify better subject.

When do you not choose the programmed setting

If the subject (or the photographer) is in motion, the programmed setting is not appropriate, because the camera could choose too long, they would not be able to properly freeze the action.

If the subject is very specific, for example if we want to photograph fireworks or artists who perform on stage, this approach suffers more or less the same automatic setup problems; the possibilities of intervention that we will have in programmed mode will not be enough to get exactly the shot you want.

In general, the shutter speed / aperture pair is always chosen from the camera and we can never get, with few controls that we will have, the rate at which we desire. If the subjects are placed at different distances from the camera and want to achieve more precise control of depth of field we will not find an ally in the exposition scheduled.

If we take a night photography where the subjects of photography are basically two, or a person in the foreground and the city lights or the sunset in the background, the programmed mode will be of no help, since only identify the subject in the foreground and, if we activated the flash will illuminate properly producing a background almost completely dark.

Shutter-priority Photography

In photography, shutter-priority, we can manually set the shutter speed and the photo room will set the aperture accordingly.

By controlling the shutter speed we can freeze action that takes place rapidly.

In the photograph priority of the times, we must focus on the shutter speed and the camera will automatically calculate on the basis of the scene lighting conditions, the value of the aperture.

The photograph at the time priority is used in all the situations in which the fundamental element of the photograph is the shutter time. The most obvious example occurs with sporting events.

With quick, you do not have time to hold the camera still and wait for the individual steps in the field of view.

We can literally track the subject with the camera and press the more significant the instant the shutter button or when the subject is well lit, or is making a particular gesture.

It is said that the subject is moving. If we take a picture from a moving vehicle, for perfectly sharp pictures we will choose the fastest time allowed by the lighting conditions.

When you choose the picture-priority

Whenever the predominant factor in the photograph is the time when we have to freeze action or when we have to choose the shortest possible time according to the lighting conditions of the scene.

When we want to choose a not a very short time, which introduces a certain amount of blur controlled, useful to accentuate the sense of movement and the dynamism of a photograph.

When do you not choose the picture-priority

If what matters is the composition of photography and precise control of depth of field, as in the portraits.

Photography Aperture-Priority

Some cameras offer the possibility of taking photographs leaving the ability to manually set the aperture of the diaphragm and thus leaving that the camera will take care to calculate the exposure time on the basis of environmental lighting conditions.

Basically what happens is that closing the diaphragm will reduce the amount of light that enters from 'objective and therefore will require a longer exposure time.

Substantially the aperture determines the depth of field of photography.

By choosing a closed diaphragm we increase the depth of field, or the amount of places subject to different distances which are simultaneously in focus in the photograph.

Opening the diaphragm instead we get a gradual reduction of depth of field, up to keep focusing only on the subject or even only the subject's eyes, while each element placed in front of or behind the subject it will be more or less out of focus.

When we choose the aperture-priority, normally we are dealing with is a subject almost. Typical examples are the portrait and a photograph of a nearby object or a "still life".

When choosing the photograph Aperture-Priority

The photograph Aperture Priority is useful when in the step we are trying to precisely control the depth of field, for example in portrait photography.

It may also be useful in the photograph of static subjects or nearly so, with a telephoto lens has a very thrust focal length.

The control of depth of field photograph guaranteed by the aperture-priority may also be useful in macro photography, when the subject is located a few centimeters, sometimes a few millimeters away from the front lens of the camera.

When do you not choose the photograph Aperture-Priority

Obviously in situations where the predominant element is time, ie in action picture, in family photos with children or animals and pictures in low light, where we can not count on a suitable support such as a tripod.

In the photos in particular lighting conditions, generally too scarce. we will try to take the picture with the shortest possible time to be able to ensure correct exposure, or at least with an underexposure not too pronounced.

Manual shooting

By manually setting the image parameters, we have complete freedom in the composition of the photograph.

Sometimes we may want to give an interpretation of reality, without limiting ourselves to photograph it as it stands.

For example, we want to accentuate the drama of a sunset using darker tones. With the setting manual we can choose a shutter speed faster or a smaller aperture and therefore obtain a more characterized photograph. The hand-held photography is suitable for all those situations where we know exactly what we want to achieve by the click and we intend to set the speed and aperture to achieve a particular effect, ignoring the indication of the exposure meter.

The manual exposure gives us more responsibility in the result of photography, as by using a manual ignore the exposure meter, or choose values that the exposure would have felt wrong. In practice we are choosing an incorrect, aware of getting a result altered compared to reality.

Generally manual setting, where provided on the camera, must be chosen for a reason and a reason in mind.

When do you not choose manual exposure

For general use, and photographs in which we do not worry too much the setting camera, choose an automatic setting.

When we have in mind a precise result in terms of shutter speed or depth of field, we choose a semi-automatic mode, the times or aperture-priority respectively.

If the lighting conditions or composition of the scene are covered by one of the programmed mode of the digital camera, we choose one of these modes and entrust ourselves to programs preset by the manufacturer.

The preset shooting modes

Most cameras offer some settings that are designed to set up the camera on a specific type of shooting.

Normally these pre settings are indicated by small icons, selectable by a ring, a button or menu option.

Of course, each camera has its own list of preset modes, which vary from model to model and from manufacturer to manufacturer.

The portrait mode

This mode, normally represented by the icon of a stylized face, intervenes substantially on the depth of field. In a portrait the aim is to isolate the subject compared to the background and any elements placed in front or behind. For this reason a diaphragm rather open is selected, which among other things allows you to use a time of rapid snap reducing risk of blurred photos. While the shutter speed is set faster than normal, to improve the exposure of the details in the subject's face.

In essence it is a setting in aperture priority, correct with shorter shutter speed, so as to produce the ideal situation for a portrait.

The landscape mode

The photographs of landscapes have one thing in common: almost always the top half of the picture is occupied by a large slice of the sky, or a large clear area in a generic Shooting Mode "would weigh too much" on the exposure choices : the camera will read the ambient light and set an appropriate shutter speed. The problem is that doing so would get a photograph without contrast, in which the sky is a pale blue, the white limit, and the ground, also because of the inevitable mist typically present in the photographs of landscapes, it will be too light and indistinct. In practice, the result will be a snap insipid, lacking in details and contrasts landscape mode alters the standard exposure by reducing a bit 'the exposure time, or take a picture slightly underexposed. In this way the blue sky will look more saturated, intense and natural and even the details of the land will be richer.

The sports mode (or children and pets)

To take pictures at sporting events or situations or dynamics to capture the small big business of children or animals we can choose the sports mode, which gives priority to shutter speed.

In practice it is a priority mode of the times, which tries to calculate the shortest shutter speed according to the ambient lighting conditions. Of course favoring the rapidity of the camera shutter speed will be forced to adopt a very open diaphragm which, especially in the photographs with tele lens, will lead to a considerable reduction also of the depth of field. This, however, is a "side effect" useful in this kind of photographs because it singled out from the background on the subject, athlete, child or animal, with the effect of focusing the viewer's gaze on the true subject of the photograph, without too many distractions.

The night photography mode

Some cameras come with a pre setting for night photography, allowing you to take pictures with a little 'extra safety in low light conditions.

The night photograph fact presents several difficulties, since the basic element of the photograph is the light; at night, for example in a large city, the light is scarce and concentrated on the street lighting lamps and the insignia of the premises. This is why the photographs of this type have specific problems: the camera reads an ambient light rather low and tends to set a slow shutter speed. This is because the camera is attempting to properly expose both the shadow areas both lights, with the result that the dark areas will result in dark gray reality and the lights are too light.

The night photography mode allows you to use a slightly shorter time to produce a deep black shadows and lights exhibited in contrasting manner, keeping intact the original colors without smudging.

Other preset modes

The various manufacturers are racing to offer certain shooting modes in their models. Normally the main modes are easily accessible, while the secondary mode provide an appropriate submenu. It is less frequently used mode, which, however, may prove useful for solving specific situations.

The important thing is to remember to have it available on your camera.

Some of them operate on the pair of shutter speed / aperture settings, by choosing it in an appropriate manner for a particular type of shutter; other act instead on the white balance, to avoid using the automatic setting that, in certain situations, it may produce erroneous results.

YOU WILL SEE THAT WITH THESE CONCEPTS REACH A SELF LEVEL FOR TAKING PHOTOS AND FUN WITH YOUR CAMERA.

GOOD JOB AND FUN.

NOTE

www.ingramcontent.com/pod-product-compliance
Lightning Source LLC
Chambersburg PA
CBHW070929220526
45468CB00005B/1708